Crossing the Waters

Also by Norita Dittberner-Jax

What They Always Were
The Watch
Longing for Home
Stopping for Breath

Crossing the Waters

poems

Norita Dittberner-Jax

NODIN PRESS

Design: John Toren
Cover photo: Jessica Larson Johnston
ISBN: 978-1-935666-98-1

Library of Congress Cataloging-in-Publication Data

Names: Dittberner-Jax, Norita, author.
Title: Crossing the waters : poems / Norita Dittberner-Jax.
Description: Minneapolis, MN : Nodin Press, [2017]
Identifiers: LCCN 2017033005 | ISBN 9781935666981
Subjects: LCSH: Amyotrophic lateral sclerosis—Poetry.
Classification: LCC PS3554.I8397 A6 2017 | DDC 811/.54—dc23. LC record available at https://lccn.loc.gov/2017033005

Nodin Press, LLC
5114 Cedar Lake Road,
Minneapolis, MN 55416

For Eugene

"What restraint or limit should there be to grief for one so dear?"
— Horace

"Then will the lame leap like a stag,
Then the tongue of the mute will sing."
-- Isaiah

A HOTEL

We've brewed the last cup
of coffee. It's time to leave
this room I've come to love
as I love all the rooms
we've slept in, this one
an interior space, purple walls
and white bed, white desk
and shutters that we opened
for the first time this morning
to find the city blurred behind grime.

You sit on the edge of the bed,
steadying yourself. I come sit
by you, side by side, our hands
cupped, looking out the window,
beyond these walls.

There are two truths –
the truth of going forward,
our reveling in the city, and
the truth of loss, of age,
your faltering, our sorrow.

Contents

I. The Pattern Lost

4   Diagnosis: Lou Gehrig's Disease
5   What I Will Miss
6   January
7   Pentimento
8   Going Through the Boxes
9   Moving Through Time
10 April
11 Leaving the Garden
12 The Pots
14 Fragments of the Summer
17 Patterns
18 Healer

II. Last Flight to Mexico

21 The Island
22 Maids
23 Expatriate
24 Riding the 2nd Class Bus
25 Madonna
26 The Yucatan
27 Retrospective: Frida in Merida
28 Mirror
29 Cane
30 Campache
31 Overnight Bus

III. Two Truths Going Forward

35 The Confluence
36 ALS Support Group
37 Saturday Morning
38 Legacy
39 Circling
40 Palm Sunday
41 City Neighborhood

42   Where I Live Now

43   Equipment

44   Bring Rock from the Garden

45   Wanting

46   The Window Facing West

47   The Kiss

48   What the Counselor Said

49   What I Do

50   Midsummer

51   The Dream of John

IV. LAMENT

55   A Psalm of Lament

56   Arrivals, Departures

57   Sunday Morning in the Old City

59   Tell Me How You Love Me

60   The Clinic Waiting Room

61   Car

62   The Wedding

63   Spring Break

64   Morning on Lake Pepin

65   But You

66   Cemetery

67   Marina

68   When leaf buds open on the trees

69   Saint Francis in the Desert

70   Family

71   Dog Shadow

72   There Are Days

73   Summer

74   In the Garden

75   Evensong

77   Acknowledgments

78   About the Author

Crossing the Waters

I

The Pattern Lost

DIAGNOSIS: LOU GEHRIG'S DISEASE

A shock so deep
the dreaming shut down,
or the memory of dreams –
half of me is dumb.

And dream's companion,
the nudge from underground
that I count on to give me
direction, where are you?

Oh, speak, other self,
have mercy, come as you do
in quiet, whisper, *come,*
follow me.

WHAT I WILL MISS

1.
You want a tabletop tree.
I try to envision it, but all I see
is the tree that reached
into the middle of the room,
or the one we wired
to the wall, or the last one
we cut ourselves, having
our Christmas fight right there
in the woods, the intensity
melting the snow around our boots.
I don't want a tabletop tree.
I feel the loss of every change
and resist, like the ice outside
that refuses to melt.

2.
Our last Christmas in this house.
How lovely it looks tonight,
almost royal, the dark oak wood,
the scarlet of the tablecloth.
Even our little tree which only
looks good in the dark, shines
like a jewel in the corner.
How to leave the fireplace,
and the oaks with their exultant
branches outside our door.

JANUARY

I read a poem by Amichai to you:
"I'll sing until my heart breaks."
The great love of the word
between us, poem, prayer,
a psalm.

Winter is here now, ice
and the hunger of the chickadees
pushed out by squirrels
at the feeder, how the world
is for them.

Inside our house, the hard edge
of your illness makes relentless
war on your body, how the world
is for you.

PENTIMENTO

Husband with folded wing, after the fall
you took on ice, I'm easing your wounded arm

into the shirt, stretching the neck over your head,
easy slide of the good arm.

Why the heaviness of this simple task,
me standing, bending, you waiting for help?

My mother, unable to dress herself, or even stand,
the permanent stasis of her left side,

long shadow of her illness.

GOING THROUGH THE BOXES

Getting ready to move,
I'm reading letters I saved,
cards and messages
from children, husbands,
the charm of well-shaped
language, and how they say it,
the handwriting of each,
a fingerprint, my mother's looped
hand for my birthday, signing
for both of them, "Love
from Mother and Dad."

I'm reading the log we kept
when she was bedridden
and he took sick, we spelled
one another and wrote it down,
medication, telephone calls,
a family crisis and comic relief.
Everything recorded, even the bottle
of Scotch brought to the family meeting.

I saved the best, and the best
has weighed me down.
I want to go lighter into the years.
What will I need for ballast against the tide
of old age? Should I save
the anniversary card of the couple
dancing with lamp shades
on their heads? We never danced
like that, but we were joyful.

MOVING THROUGH TIME

While the coffee brews,
I stare out the window
at the snow graying,
winter's end.

Sparrows cross the yard,
a host of them, lighting
on the eaves, and I wonder
how they all agree.

They live here, thanks
to the lilac bushes and the neighbor's
fir tree, good for hiding
from the hawk.

Smoke billows from a chimney
chugging into polar air
above a mountain peak of roof.
Smoke and sparrows on the lam.

APRIL

Always a miracle
when the cold relents
and spring is possible.
Good news from the doctor
after our long winter,
and it seems we could go on
forever, spring following winter,
good news after bad, so
ready to believe anything
as long as morning comes.

LEAVING THE GARDEN

We should have moved in winter
when there's nothing
for the eye, the garden reduced
to root, tuber, not now
when the life of plants pushes up
and out, the third day
of creation, so good, all good.

We have lived in beauty,
cultivated it, the slender grasses,
the curly crab,
lily-of-the-valley everywhere
flaunting my failure
to arrange them as I wish.

Along the garage, where
snow-on-the-mountain grows wild,
I planted petunias of
deepest scarlet and set small
stones from Superior,
a narrow line of beauty.

Why curse the Jane Austen rose,
that only blossomed the first year
though I fed and pruned it,
checking it each morning.

Hosta, the rhubarb, sexual again,
peonies, and how to leave
the bleeding heart, especially
the white one, tiny bells shifting in wind.

THE POTS

These huge clay pots, upside down
on the lawn, will not hold calla lilies
this year, no afternoons
of you bending to fill them with soil
and rhizomes you stored all winter.

Summer after summer, pots
of jungle spears in June
brought forth blossoms of lemon
and a white so creamy I wanted
to wrap myself in its elegant shawl.

One summer we hauled the pots
to the front stoop and posed leggy
grandchildren, all skinned knees
in front of them so they looked
like fairy children sprouting flowers.

Another year, after we traveled in Italy,
we lined them up by the garage
to remind us of the orderly beauty
of Italian trees. Now the pots
are upside down on the lawn

like bells without clangers.
Who comes for the pots?
Our children, grown to love flowers
as we do, neighbors who will
miss the back and forth of garden talk.

The hosta are up, boxwood survived.
What use to watch them grow?
I stay inside sorting and packing,
as we prepare to leave. You're quieter
these days, wanting your pots.

FRAGMENTS OF THE SUMMER

1.
After the move, I pick up
the pieces, count the keys
to the new place
with its many locks.

The car littered, my purse stuffed
with receipts, bills of ladling.
A hundred dislocations, ungrounded,
I'm floating.

2.
The stories are almost all the same: sudden
death of a spouse, children fly in,
find a new place for the one left.

I have twisted the worry rag of your death
for years. Our new neighbors,
the ones that were left, tell their stories
at breakfast without flinching,
the tale smooth, the fracture mended,
isn't it?

3.
Bird song wakes me. Your hand
curls around mine in sleep.

4.
Every day new signs
of the disease.
Will your body never
leave you
alone?

5.
The sun is high and never sets.
A hot wind, as if we were still
in Mexico, straining against sun,
weathered.

Light so sharp, I see the wear
on the dining room chairs,
the years of darkening
and where are my oak trees?

6.
If I hadn't moved here, I would never
know the intricacy of changing
billboards, the science of hinges
and pulleys as the driver hoists
the basket carrying one man to the top.
He starts unfastening in perfect
time to the man on the ledge. They
fold the old and down comes the spaceman,
Are you ready? I turn my back
and they're smoothing
We Are Hmong with their brushes.

Trivia from the new place
that I will keep along with the exact
time school let out on Goodrich,
the progress of elm disease on Lombard,
back to firecrackers exploding
on the streetcar tracks on Thomas Avenue.

7.
A road trip to relatives.
In the rush to pack,
to leave the city,
I speed down
country roads passing
acres of corn fields on either
side. For a minute
I think I should be doing
something about the corn.

8.
A small town is a good place
for trees. I don't mean the chorus
of them crowding the hills.
I mean the one in the big yard
with the truck in the driveway,
that splendid beauty that greets you
as you round the curve,
a tree allowed to breathe, to grow
under the *best* conditions: sun,
rain, air, room.

9.
An urgency, not enough
time because time
is running out, the stream
of sand through the hour glass,
one-half empty, the other,
complete, at rest.

10.
Living with sickness, the light around us,
the closeness, like the icons,
a mandorla of light.

PATTERNS

How often now I go alone
where we once went together,
the pattern lost, the way home
devoid of laughter at antics
we saw, and arriving, no need
to check the machine, the beep
of the outside world,
 "There's a message."

Now, I close and lock doors
against the dark, walk into the light
of you reading in your red chair.
You look up and smile, "How was it?"
I tell you, then we go to bed,
the same bed, a blessing.

HEALER

Seeing you in pain in your chair,
I think of the hour we spent
with the healer in San Cristobal.
For an offering of 40 pesos, he prayed
over you. As he struck you
with a sword of basil,
you pointed to the small of your back
where the devil resides,
wanting relief from the pain.
I bring what I have—pills and water
and a fig for sweetness.

II

Last Flight to Mexico

THE ISLAND

Our *casa* was simple and elegant. The courtyard where the
internet worked was next to the open air where rain
dripped off the awning and wind swayed the palm trees.
The only appointments: one lemon tree, two chaise lounges, and
three spiky plants in identical pots. Someone arranged all that
for us. What wasn't arranged was the Caribbean on our side
of the island, the tide wild and unsafe, held back only by the
seawall where we walked each morning.

MAIDS

Sheets changed, tile scrubbed every day,
small, brown women appeared and disappeared
behind doors, holding the hotel together,
piecing it like a garment, in and out.

I saw them in the stairway with their bundles
of sheets and towels, burdened as the sellers
on the street, the store on their backs.
They never took the elevator.

I took the steps to offset the *guacamole,*
the *huevos,* the way I never eat at home.
The maids so lean, wiry, moving
silently with mops and pails

except when they greeted me on the landing.
"*Buenos dias,*" they said to me. "*Buenos dias.*"

EXPATRIATE

Margaritas salty and cold
around the table. We tried
one subject after another,
searching for connection.
A few left for the kitchen
for the strong medicine
that Charles served up.
It's ten years since he left
Baltimore to run a hotel here.
He likes to keep his guests
cocooned, breakfast heavy
with *huevos* and *frejoles*,
plates of melon and pineapple,
the best coffee. A few hours
free before happy hour,
then roof-top to see stars
over the Caribbean.
When he asked us where
we would be staying next,
he said of the hotel, "*Very*
Mexican."

RIDING THE 2ND CLASS BUS

We left the island,
drove into the interior,
vast scrub brush,
roofs thick with thatch,
abandoned cars.

In the middle of the road,
drop-offs, pick ups.
Unscheduled stops.
Impatient, I watched
the time, then stopped myself.
We rumbled off.

How life is lived: a woman
hangs clothes on a crooked
line and though the sun
is high and hot, a man
in a long-sleeved shirt
walks a dirt road with his dog.

MADONNA

Unlike her son, she does not suffer.
Nothing in her face reveals
her legendary sorrow. She is mother,
goddess, Our Lady of Soledad, Our Lady
of Guadalupe. In the Metropolitan Cathedral,
the very pillars are sheathed in velvet
for her feast day, and in the villages
streamers festoon the trees. But the poor
love her best. No running water
and the cooking shed covered with corrugated
tin, but one whole wall for her statue.
A profusion of candles in deep red glasses,
the rotten and burned-out right next
to the new, as if this multiplicity could stem
a flood of trouble coming down from the mountains,
as if there were protection in the candor
of rotting flowers.

THE YUCATAN

In colonial towns the cathedral
borders the square, a formality
like the *parques* themselves,
plantings of vegetation, wild sage,
salvia, winding paths leading
to the bandstand in the center,
but at the edges, *confidentiales,*
love seats, white and curved
like the throats of swan,
and palm trees painted white
half-way up the trunks, and the trunks
entwined as our limbs were hours ago.

RETROSPECTIVE: FRIDA IN MERIDA

*"I hope the exit is joyful—and I hope never
to return."*

— Frida Kahlo

In our hotel, posters of her paintings
line the walls of the lobby. On the way
to the elevator, baby Diego in her arms.

Every painting, a mirror, her life of pain
after the accident. She is queen
of Mexico now, Frida of the unibrow.

Her face makes money —
on Bohemia's *cerveza*, special edition,
her face on a decorative frying pan.

The government has forgiven her affair
with Trotsky and put her face
on the $500 peso bill,

Diego in the dust, far from the catwalk
that connected their houses,
the wheelchair, death mask still in place.

When I stood on the corner in Merida
buses careening, engines revved,
it's her damaged body that haunted me —

stand back, she said to me,
stand back.

MIRROR

They were walking home after dinner when they saw a barber
shop. The hair in his ears needed trimming and the back of
his neck was shaggy. The barber wanted to keep watching the
soccer game on television, but offered a chair. No language on
either side. She tried to indicate with gestures the ear hair, but
the barber thought she meant to cut the beard. Her husband
gave her the eye and she butted out, retreating to a chair to
rifle through the men's magazines with pictures of scantily clad
women. She looked up once at her husband's face in the mirror.
She saw that he was old. Not the lively face she lived with,
walking or talking or sitting quietly next to each other. She
looked down at the magazine but didn't turn any more pages.
When the barber swung the chair around and her husband
walked toward her, she saw that he was vigorous and polished
in his new haircut and the *guayabera* shirt, all white linen.

CANE

The sidewalks of Merida were narrow and I often walked ahead
of Gene, listening for the tap-tap-tap of his cane. One day he
asked me to walk behind him and I got mad. To me it seemed an
ancient gender practice for the woman to walk behind the man,
never ahead, never leading. He said it was wrong of me to not take
account of his hardship, that he pushes himself painfully to keep
up. I was confused. Should I fight with him or take care of him?
After that, I consciously slowed my natural movements and walked
behind him. What I saw startled me. How painfully he maneuvered
his way forward, how rickety his body had become over the course
of our trip. Sometimes I unconsciously forgot and moved ahead
before I caught myself and pulled back. I didn't want to see.

CAMPACHE, MEXICO

After dinner, we walked the seawall
built to ward off pirates,
the cannon pointing out
on the open waters of the Gulf,
when you were a wealthy city,
Campache.

Past the exercisers who stretch
and bend to marimbas,
past skateboarders, lovers,
the *malecon* gathered us all in.

We walked too far. Turning back,
the music was gone, the *malecon* deserted,
except for a lone runner
behind us, breathing hard.

I thought twilight would last.

How did they bear up, pirates, sailors
what promise of gold lured them
through the abyss?

The sea and the darkness –
I was so close to the water.

OVERNIGHT BUS

Next to me, you slept,
like the others

snoring softly,
legs sprawled in the aisle,

only the driver
and I awake.

He was making good time,
a long stretch

with no stops,
no human habitation.

I pulled open the curtain –
Stars, a skyful,

of stars, above
and all the way

to the horizon,
the joy of stars

without number,
but fear, too

of the immensity.
We coursed

through the darkness,
I'd never been

where we were going,
never ridden the night bus

getting there.

III

Two Truths Going Forward

THE CONFLUENCE

On the bridge, heading home
from my errands, I see Pike Island,
a verdant arrow of land
where the waters of the Minnesota River
flow into the Mississippi.

The Dakota thought this point sacred,
the center of the earth.

We moved here because of the sickness.
but in the glory of autumn light,
the world is new, water
and land, primeval.

Long or short, this is our time
at the river.

When I walk the river trail,
the ground that they walked,
I remember and ask the ancients
to help us take strength
from the rivers.

Our time here is sacred.
We live in a holy place.

ALS Support Group

The other men have been silenced
by the disease, most in wheelchairs,
not you, not yet.

The respiratory therapist shows us
six different machines for clearing
the throat, for easier breathing,
and finally for forcing
the breath itself.

I'm quiet, new here, wondering,
will I be fierce enough,
like Joan for her Ted,
or Susan for Mike,
so young, eager to show us
the feeding tube in his stomach.

Silent in the car, too,
we are tired, heading home.

SATURDAY MORNING

and the radio is playing music from the movies,
MGM, and *Brigadoon* sweeps into
the kitchen like the fog in that opening scene.
I turn the volume up and hear my sister,
dead three years now, playing, "Come to me,
bend to me," and those four rising chords,
"kiss me good day," and I've stopped
clearing up breakfast, I'm back with her
at the piano, how we loved that music,
she played it and we sang and I always
knew all the words, and the remembering
is so strong that I'm in tears when my husband
comes into the kitchen and I know he's going to say
it's too loud, but he sees how it is with me
and I say, "Mary Lou," and he nods and kisses
my forehead and still wants me to turn it down.

LEGACY

after Beth Kephart

I come from music. The poems beat
with the pulse of my father's baritone,
the strokes of piano keys, merry and sad.

I come from my mother's intelligence
and humor, that slight distance in outlook,
the wry aside – I carry now.

I come from the passion of his voice rising
against union busters, her delight in the sound
of words and children.

And flowers – morning glories by the back porch,
explaining themselves in the faces of lilies,
delphinium, the order of the garden.

I come from my mother and father, their passions
explain me, anger at injustice, tulips on the table,
the music under poems, praise today, only praise.

CIRCLING

What will winter here
has already moved in.

The lines of poems I wrote
thirty years ago
come back to me now in the same
circumstances that inspired them,

A few trees left
on the spine of the hills,
black-sleeved arms
fingering the dark.

A shadow close by, a sense
that it will abide.

I'm circling back,
taking my years with me,
that great robe of time
circling my shoulders.

PALM SUNDAY

A lax Catholic, but here I am
in church, surprised that the statues
are shrouded in purple for Lent,
just as they were when I was a girl
at St. Vincent's.

We read Matthew's passion,
the priest is Jesus, the head usher,
the narrator; we in the congregation
take the chorus parts. "Barabas,"
we say, "Crucify him,"
with fervor as thin as the pages
of the missal.

Toward the end, Matthew writes,
the veil of the temple was torn
in two; the tombs opened
and the bodies of holy men and women
rose from the dead.

That's when I missed you, Mexico.
I know in your mountain churches
there's a tableau of saints rising
out of their deaths, dazed, dazzled
and people on their knees
singing in tongues.

CITY NEIGHBORHOOD

Its houses and gardens shaped
the architecture of my days,
porches, the front stoop,
the way I lived and thought,
the juxtaposition of light and stone,
weeds, blossom. In my mind
I'm still walking its sidewalks
from one house to another.

WHERE I LIVE NOW

The grass is flawless and traffic
on the bridge over the Mississippi
flows with the constancy
of the river itself.

No houses but across the highway
trees, thousands of them.

One day I found a grove of cottonwoods
murmuring together; I sat down
on a log to listen.

There's a river birch outside the balcony
exactly the size of the one I left
two moves ago. A joy, though it will unfold
slower than I will age or you falter.

EQUIPMENT

Deluxe walker, awkward
as a small dinosaur
in our living room,
manual wheelchair, power
wheelchair to come,
paperwork, 18 pages.
A wedge for easier breathing,
gastric tube and its plugs,
gauze bandages, beaker
and syringe, bi-pap machine,
distilled water, the mask
and its proboscis, three
canes, bed rail and
the handicapped sign.

I hide the equipment,
won't let it make any more
inroads than necessary,
even as you lose one
function after another.
When the end comes
these things will remain,
what I cannot love.

I want a private event
after the funeral, just me
and the things in an isolated
spot where, like a witch,
I will burn the combustibles.
Then with the unholy strength
I'm building, I'll hurl the rest
in defiance over a cliff
into the deep.

BRING ROCK FROM THE GARDEN

Sky, river, light.
Where will we put the porcelain sparrow?
Peace in our old house, peace
in the new.
Beloved face, tender marsh,
stay with me. The dread opens
at my feet.

WANTING

I run into people I thought
were friends who haven't called us;
they ask about your condition.

I tell them.

Silence. Maybe they didn't
understand. I try again
to close the gap.

Why don't they say something?

We go our ways, traffic resumes
but there is a chasm where
I wanted a bridge.

Is no one going to scream?

Do I have to hire a keener
to mouth the grief?
I want someone to scream.

When I tell the counselor this,
she says the scream
is in me, but I don't yet
have the language.

THE WINDOW FACING WEST

The sweet low light of November
envelops the room
turning the desk bronze.

How can losing the light be sweet?
How can the waning days
of your strength be tender?

Do Not Resusitate.
Do Not Intubate.
Your directive in the drawer.

In the stillness of late afternoon
I sit in the chair alone, as I will be.
You are gone for only an hour,

but I am trying on your death.
The traffic on the bridge is steady,
the passing of cars heading home.

Now the sun rests on the trees.
The bronze of the desk fades. The door
of your return clicks open.

THE KISS

At the graduation, people ask about you
or don't.

Later, you say when I leave the house I forget
to kiss you.

Are you becoming invisible
to me?

I would rather forget
my name.

After I am sad and pondering the meaning,
I think,

he misses
my kisses

reminding me of our losing each other
at the Dead Sea resort

you had an announcer summon me;
you were mad

and I was happy, knowing you would never
leave me behind.

WHAT THE COUNSELOR SAID

Only seconds, but timeless,
my life after you're gone,
the loss of ground, falling off
the great cliff into
nothing,

then snap back,
where I'm turning
out the lights,
shutting down the apartment.

She said the void is real but
there will be tiny parachutes
to help me. I picture them orange
in the black sky.

She said it would happen again,
but what's important
is coming back to the moment,
the rumpled covers, your steady
breathing.

WHAT I DO

I'm sorting and cleaning
your closet
so it's easy to dress.
I'm throwing away
the shirt I loved
and you didn't,
packing them up
for the Goodwill.
I'm busy, managing
things that can be boxed,
sorted, arranging
the furniture of the future
without considering
the future, ignoring
the river outside the door
but I hear traffic
on the bridge coming
and going at high speed,
as I rush back and forth
from one end
of the apartment
to the other,
far above the current.

MIDSUMMER

In my new life,
I'm finding places to walk
alongside the Mississippi,
among joggers and bikers
who zip past me.

Last evening, we went together,
you with the walker
with its basket and seat.
The air was soft against
our skin. An egret in the woods
spread its wings.

Let's walk tomorrow, too,
and next week. This is the summer
we have, no promise
of next year, just this life,
hummingbirds and books,
and the ample light
of July.

An ease,
gold, the sun,
green of high summer,
the tug of the old
gives way.

THE DREAM OF JOHN

Gone, seven years. Last night in sleep
I conjured my brother
back from the dead.

He wore a robe and was
speaking out against war
as he did in his lifetime.

We embraced so naturally,
he in his fullness
before the wasting.

I woke buoyant, so glad,
for my vision, the capacity
to conjure what is gone.

My brother John came back
on his best day, his body easy,
his mind clear.

How much more you, husband,
whom I have known from the blackest of hair
to the white head I saw yesterday

from a distance, you with the walker,
crossing the portico and I thought, who is
that man with the beautiful hair?

You will come back to me.
I will take the shards of memory
and forge you in the furnace

of my awful desire that you live.

IV.
Lament

A PSALM OF LAMENT

Lord, I watch him falter each day,
his body a cage of bones. Have you
forgotten him? Is he *in* your care?
How long will he suffer disease?
You stayed with me through perils
of mind and heart, even as I
ignored you in happy times
and was just happy, but hear me now.
Stay with him. Stay with me.
Bring what comfort you have.
You gave him a mind bright as fire,
a heart soft for suffering,
our life together a balm. And even
as I ask, "how long?" I would not
lessen his life for one day if it were
mine to do. Whatever time is ours
I want, take him in your time.
Give us patience to endure,
enough forgetfulness to love
only the day we have, the night
to feel the other turn in sleep

Arrivals, Departures

What wouldn't I do for you now, husband,
grounded as you are to the house.
I might have seen London, Paris, but Istanbul?
Jerusalem? Brazil? Those I owe to you.
First you led, so easy with strangers,
then I found my footing in the world,
and we climbed side by side up the hill
to mosque, cathedral, temple, walked
the honeyed cobbles of the Old City,
stood at the Wailing Wall and slipped the names
of the beloved in the stone.

What wouldn't I do for you now?

SUNDAY MORNING IN THE OLD CITY

*"For the peace of Jerusalem pray: may peace reign in your walls,
in your palaces, peace!"* Psalm 121

I.
Through olive groves and the amphitheatre where rock bands
blasted the night, we climbed to Jaffa gate into the Old City,

the grated shops with their gunnysacks plump with almonds
and lentils, casks of jewelry, tunics and rugs hanging like
laundry, waiting

for the hot breath of the bargaining to come. Quiet as thieves
and as quick, we passed under a canopy of lush bougainvillea,
and heard the cry

of a baby, the clink of silverware, the interior life above the
shops; past the Church of the Holy Sepulchre, the cavernous
vault

eerie with the glow of red votives, wax from a thousand
candles, past the narrow checkpoint where Israeli soldiers
inspected our bags before

we entered the plaza of the Wailing Wall, where we stood
with the Jews yesterday, touching our foreheads to the stone,

up to the summit where the golden Dome of the Rock
shines over all Jerusalem.

II.
Jerusalem, Jerusalem
the very name embedded as fossil in my mind,
ancient stone, city of the psalms,

"Jerusalem, My Happy Home,"
the hymn we sang at my mother's funeral,

Jerusalem, where all the streets
are a Via Dolorosa,

Jerusalem, crossroads of traffic with the divine,
mystical city

where Abraham lay wood to make human sacrifice
of his only child,

where Mohammed mounted
the ladder to heaven,

where the Jews gather
at their holiest site to pray at the one wall
remaining of Temple Mount.

I walked the esplanade, looking out over the city,
the blindingly white stone,
of modern Jerusalem on one side,
on the other, the Garden of Gethsemane
where Jesus prayed for courage
and the bleached gravestones
of two millennia shine in the morning sun.

I stood on the ramparts
like the ancients looking out over
the whole known world.

TELL ME HOW YOU LOVE ME

The first memory, the dearest
gift, tell me all the details
so I can store them up,
against the erosion
of our common life, so much
losing.

In my dreams, I lose keys,
lose the car and wake relieved
that my accoutrements
are still here.

One night I dreamt I lost
my poems, a sign so serious,
I didn't tell you.

THE CLINIC WAITING ROOM

We're waiting for the next appointment, the one in which
they'll measure you, sooner than we expected, for a motorized
wheelchair. You're tired, but I'm still on high alert, measuring
doorways in my head, picturing myself driving a van, high
up and you behind me when our whole life has been side
by side. The other couple in the waiting room is older than
we are, he hoisted back in his wheelchair, she by his side,
taking his scarf and gloves, nodding to us pleasantly. She is
slight, gray hair combed back, two black barrettes holding it
in place girlishly. Curious, you ask them if they have a van.
The man nods his head. "Chrysler," he says, his voice harsh,
as if it's carried on barbed wire. She smiles. "I prefer to be a
passenger, but I've gotten used to driving it," she says. She
has distilled her history in that remark, her satisfaction in her
gender and the dignity with which she embraces the change
required. Her husband, responsive even as words are slow to
come, says, "She   does   very   well."

CAR

The car is totaled from the accident.
We called Al. He's aged since
the last car, but he's buoyant.

Al leaves to finish the paperwork
on the new car, Basque red, which is no
red at all. I wait, looking out the window
where the new car is purring.

It is a beautiful car
and what American is not
happy about a new car?

You've gone home, leaving me
to close the deal. When I was upset
about the accident, you said,
"We can't be concerned about
those things now."

Not so different from our first date,
when you picked me up
in a small station wagon
with a cookie tin on the floor,
driver's side, to keep the rain out.

When Al comes back, I sign
the contract, and it is only
my signature. The aching absence
of your name makes me forlorn.
This the car of my widowhood.

THE WEDDING

Let me say how much I've loved going out
with you, the two of us, a couple.

I've creased your trousers and ironed the blue shirt
that colors your pale skin. That little section

of wrist below the cuff that drives me crazy in a man
drives me crazy now. I've misted the air

with perfume and walked through it
the way French women do.

I have on "eyes" as my mother would say, and
sterling silver at my wrist.

You're tired and your arms hurt, supporting yourself
on the walker, but I know you will relish

greeting people, a social man, you'll laugh, full-throated
again. People will say to one another,

"He still looks good," and you do. This wedding,
the granddaughter of old friends, may be our last.

Soon I'll stop trying so hard to keep the old life.
We'll both give in to the disease, just not yet.

We look as good as we're ever going to look,
and the sun is unexpectedly warm for March.

Out we go.

SPRING BREAK

On our first wheelchair excursion overnight, the weather was
spectacular, the first nice weekend after winter. Some things
were hard in a town as old as Stillwater. We learned that the
term "handicapped accessible" is a broad term, which often
means a rickety ramp that begins in the back by the trash
receptacles.

We didn't expect the motorcycle festival, the constant gun
or motors crossing the Saint Croix River, hair-flying women
holding onto stern men at the controls, pilots without a
plane. We saw prom couples, one young woman in a strapless
dress, hitching up the bodice before photos, her date, just a
boy in a tux. Two different wedding parties took turns posing
at the bandstand. They danced late into the night on the
ground floor of our hotel.

Gene drove his wheelchair right through the muddle of all
this, with me behind him enjoying the spectacle, so far from
the hissing oxygen machine and the green cord snaking
through our apartment.

Morning on Lake Pepin

The lake is a bowl
of quiet, its depth hidden.
Trees at the rim, sky
wide, uncluttered.

The lake is an offering
of hands cupped,
a gift.

Give yourself
to the openness of water,
sky, stone, tree.

This is what you have,
the gift of quiet after sleep,
disturbed sleep.

The simplicity of elements,
the dream lake.

But You

I dreamed
I was opening
the door
to friends.
I was pink
with health
and wore
a blouse
that fit me
like a skin.
Behind me
the table
was set –
the fragrance
of spices
ingeniously
concocted
filled the
apartment.
I had every
thing I loved.

CEMETERY

On the Sunday before Memorial Day, we went to Oakland
Cemetery where we have two graves. Next to our lot is the
grave of my former student, William, who went down with
Paul Wellstone's plane. Above our site is a finely carved angel
high on her pedestal. The grounds in their summer glory were
splendid. Why hadn't I noticed before that Oakland Cemetery
is full of oak trees, the tree that has given me the most comfort?
I heard once that the whole area of Saint Paul had once been a
savannah of oaks, reduced now to smaller patches like Oakland
Cemetery. It made me happy that Gene will be among the oaks
and that I will join him there. We drove around and found
the most direct entrance to our plot, so we won't get lost on
the curving paths. Enter on Sycamore and take the 2nd right.
On the way home, Gene told me he wanted to lie down on
our spot, but thought it was too odd an idea and besides, he
couldn't have gotten back up.

MARINA

The sun burns low over the hills,
its brilliance a distortion from
a Canadian blaze, but it's magic to me,
walking the quay, you with your walker,
after a perfect dinner.

Out on the lake, sailboats make
their lovely geometry, others
moored like stick men in the harbor.

We pass a couple on a bench,
Saturday night, no work tomorrow,
oh, the possibilities.

Toward the end of the quay,
we see three guys fishing from the rocks,
blues on the radio. I haven't
heard music in days.

One of them is singing in a rich baritone,
he turns, holding his arm out,
inviting us into his moment.

You rest on the seat of the walker.
I rest my hands on your shoulders.
We laugh.

WHEN LEAF BUDS OPEN ON THE TREES

a soft green appears and if it rains then,
hard, the young leaves drink it in without
hesitation, and even the bark of the most
ordinary tree is erotic, dark after rain.

The branches stand out, outlined in black
like my childhood drawings, an early
fascination with structure, with contrast,
the bark against the shine of leaves.

Even when the trees bush out, fulsome
with leaves, it stays with me,
the intricate fretwork, the road clear
right up to the top, the tree revealing itself.

SAINT FRANCIS IN THE DESERT

Drawn into the strange light
that turned the rocky cliff jade green,

Francis left the grotto, his sandals,
the skull perched above the book of Holy Writ.

In the field nearby, a young donkey sees it, too.
Everything faces immanent light except the hare,

so plump, content to remain close to the friar's
wooly cloak. All the elements of life, clouds,

Sister Water from the spout, Brother Heron nearby
are present as Francis stands transfixed,

arms wide, his torso, his whole body
a triptych of reverence, of transformation.

If you look closely, you can see the stigmata
on his hands and that's the heavenly Jerusalem

in the background, but the force of the painting
is Francis in radiance. This is more than technique.

Bellini knew this state or he could not have painted
Francis full-strength in the sway of it,

so that whatever the viewer brings to the painting,
coming upon it, as I did and stopped to tears,

we want, like Brother Hare, to stand with Francis.

[The Frick Museum, New York City]

FAMILY

Awake, in the middle of the night
I think of my brother's family
not seen since his funeral
and my sister's family not seen
since she died. The loss comes to me
as a great shearing, cutting
a wide swath, layer after layer
of family gone, the terrible
winnowing out, the thinning.

I want them all back,
as we were, lively, troubled,
generous or not, I want us
to laugh and sing again,
this oversized family with no
house big enough to hold us
so we gathered in summer
at the picnic or at weddings
and now at funerals of which
even one is too many.

DOG SHADOW

Is it the ghost of my stepdog,
long dead, or fear
of being left alone?

I already know her name, *Roxie.*
Her eyes will look up at me
with such attention.

She is my spirit dog,
one who will stay with me
doggedly to my almost end.

THERE ARE DAYS

One morning, feeling strong, you wanted
to go shopping, so I fired up Big Mama,
you rolled up the ramp and off we went
to the mall, up and down Macy's aisles,
toddlers staring at you. I stopped to look
at things and turned to find you gone,
but heard the click of your wheelchair,
just as I heard the click of your cane
in Mexico. At Macy's I found skinny jeans
in the right size for our skinny grandson
and waited in line behind a woman buying
a whole pile of little girl clothes. Her child,
deadpan, finger in her mouth, watched you,
how sweet you seemed, me not-so-sweet,
still at check-out. The clerk rang up the grand
total and the customer began to subtract.
Even with coupons, she didn't have the money.
I looked away to where you and the child
had come to an arrangement, you, playful,
showing her your turns, she interested.
On the way home, I was quiet, thinking
of that mother when you told me,
"That little girl thought I was a magic figure,
half-man, half-car."

SUMMER

When the rains come,
oak bark blackens to a bold
calligraphy, small tufts
of leaves fall, an afterthought.

The peonies we picked
before the downpour
bend in fullness before
the letting go begins.

Oak and peony,
and what of our arms
which narrow
to the tender bones of wrist
before widening to hands
that hold and let go,
hold and then let go.

IN THE GARDEN

The great frond of rhubarb dwarfs
Mexican heather.
The rabbit eats the only rose
that survived the winter.

Life! Life!

EVENSONG

Walking the river trail,
I see one boat, one fisherman
on the river, his back
against low sun.
I think of the Dakota,
the early ones in their river
solitude, knowing the currents
and when to head to shore.
Darkness narrows the river's
silver path. I'm heading
home myself, up the steep hill,
a little breathless. A chill
from the woods touches my arm.
How we come to evening.

ACKNOWLEDGMENTS

Many people have helped us in the course of this disease. Foremost is the VA's Amyotrophic Lateral Sclerosis (ALS) clinic whose breadth and depth of support for both of us is extraordinary. The great competence and generosity of the staff makes this illness bearable. To my fellow caregivers, meeting with you is a delight. I am grateful for your wisdom and resilience, to say nothing of the hundred tips you have for managing life in a wheelchair.

Family and friends have given us food, flowers, they've kept us company, done errands, fixed technological contraptions, attended difficult meetings, filled the bird feeders, and brought many gifts of chocolate. Praise be.

I wrote many of these poems in a white heat after the diagnosis of ALS and the upheaval of moving because of it. Thank you to poets Margaret Hasse and Sharon Chmielarz for insight into shaping the poems and the book, as well as to John Toren, gifted designer for Nodin Press. To Publisher Norton Stillman, my deep gratitude for believing in these poems and bringing them to publication.

Some of these poems appeared in the following publications for which I am grateful: *Commonweal, Whistling Shade, Hamilton Stone Review, Albuquerque Review, Poetry East, Sleet Magazine,* and *Boomer Lit.*

Finally, thank you to my husband, Eugene, for the openness and spirit with which he lives out his days. To keep him company is a gift.

About the Author

Norita Dittberner-Jax was born and raised in the Frogtown neighborhood of Saint Paul, the sixth of seven children. She was educated in parochial schools and graduated from the (then) College of Saint Catherine. After her first marriage and the birth of three children, she began to write poetry, just as the Twin Cities area was becoming a center for creative writing with the emergence of the Loft. She taught English in the public schools of Saint Paul, and creative writing for the Writers-in-the Schools Program and at the Perpich Center for the Arts. Her second marriage to Eugene Jax brought international travel and a great interest in art. In retirement from teaching, she returned to academic life, earning an MFA in poetry from Hamline University. Norita is one of the poetry editors for Red Bird Chapbooks. *Crossing the Waters* is her fifth collection of poems.